JOHN 'JOCK' FINDLAY was born in 1915, t
eldest sister, Elizabeth, died in infancy. H
and then went on to serve an apprentices
with the Pumpherston Oil Company. He married Helen 'Lena' Johnston
and the couple had twin boys, Ian and Leonard. After the war, he spent
time working in the Middle East in the newly developing oil industry.
Not long after he returned he lost his leg in a road accident. Undeterred
by this, he worked at his trade up until his retirement. Jock was a skilled
craftsman and enjoyed making and fixing things and working around the
house and garden. He enjoyed travelling, reading, the odd bet on a horse
and a nice glass of whisky. He is survived by his son Leonard, who still
lives in Pumpherston.

This book has been transcribed from Jock's memoirs by his grandson Neil.
Special thanks are due to Robin Chesters at the Almond Valley Heritage
Trust for his help in sourcing photographs, to the Trust for giving permission
to use them and to Sybil Cavanagh for her support and excellent contribution
to this project.

Life in the Raws

Memories of a Shale Oil Village

JOCK FINDLAY

with NEIL FINDLAY and SYBIL CAVANAGH

Luath Press Limited

EDINBURGH

www.luath.co.uk

First published 2020

ISBN: 978-1-910022-12-2

The author's right to be identified as author of this book
under the Copyright, Designs and Patents Act 1988 has been asserted.

The paper used in this book is recyclable. It is made
from low chlorine pulps produced in a low energy,
low emission manner from renewable forests.

Printed and bound by Bell & Bain Ltd, Glasgow

Typeset in 12 point Sabon
by Main Point Books, Edinburgh

This book is dedicated to my Granda' Jock,
my Granny Lena and my Aunty Mary Wynne (Jock's sister)
and to Pumpherston and the shale industry –
all have had a huge and lasting influence on my life.

Contents

John 'Jock' Findlay Family Tree

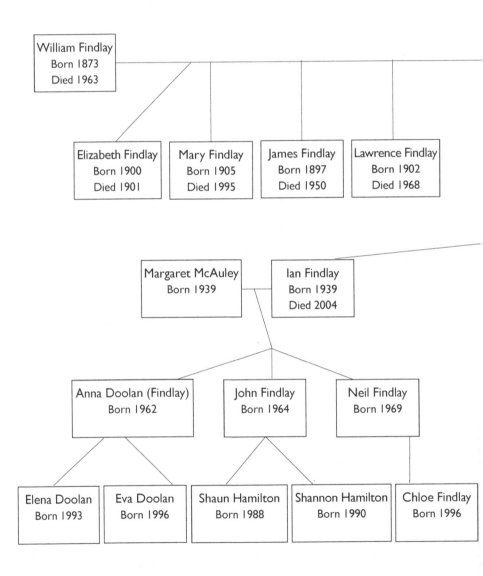

William Findlay
Born 1873
Died 1963

Elizabeth Findlay
Born 1900
Died 1901

Mary Findlay
Born 1905
Died 1995

James Findlay
Born 1897
Died 1950

Lawrence Findlay
Born 1902
Died 1968

Margaret McAuley
Born 1939

Ian Findlay
Born 1939
Died 2004

Anna Doolan (Findlay)
Born 1962

John Findlay
Born 1964

Neil Findlay
Born 1969

Elena Doolan
Born 1993

Eva Doolan
Born 1996

Shaun Hamilton
Born 1988

Shannon Hamilton
Born 1990

Chloe Findlay
Born 1996

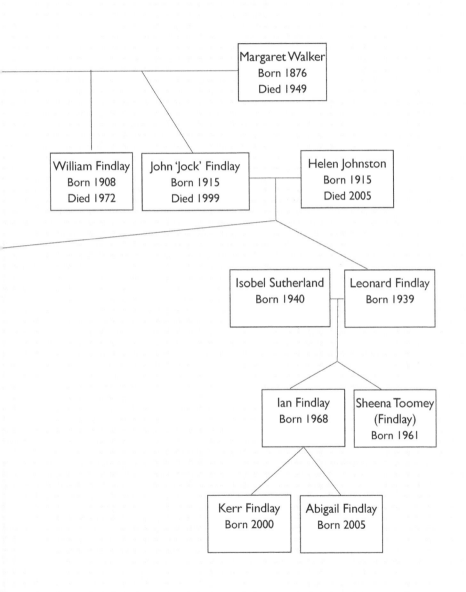

Margaret Walker
Born 1876
Died 1949

William Findlay
Born 1908
Died 1972

John 'Jock' Findlay
Born 1915
Died 1999

Helen Johnston
Born 1915
Died 2005

Isobel Sutherland
Born 1940

Leonard Findlay
Born 1939

Ian Findlay
Born 1968

Sheena Toomey
(Findlay)
Born 1961

Kerr Findlay
Born 2000

Abigail Findlay
Born 2005

Jock showing his
domestic skills

Ian and Leonard aged 21

The People Who Made This Book

JOHN 'JOCK' FINDLAY was born and brought up in the heart of the burgeoning West Lothian shale oil industry. His family and working life were shaped and dominated by the Pumpherston Oil Company or 'the works' as it was known locally. 'The works' provided jobs, housing, education, cultural events, sport and recreation.

Jock was educated at the local primary school before following other members of his family into the oil industry, working as an apprentice and tradesman chemical plumber; a job which saw him later spread his wings, with a spell in the Middle East. In his early 20s, he suffered very serious injuries following a motorbike accident, which resulted in him spending a year in hospital and ultimately losing his leg. He returned to work determined that his disability would not hinder him – it never did. He worked up to retirement age, travelled widely and was always occupied in his garden, his shed or the workshop in the old wash house at his home in the South Village raws.

Jock and his wife Lena had twin boys, Ian (Neil's father, now deceased) and Leonard, who still lives in the village. It was Leonard, as the Chief Electrician at the BP detergent works which occupied the site of the former Pumpherston oil works, who turned off the power and was the last man out when the plant closed in 1993, thus ending over a century of Findlay family connections to oil and chemical processing in the village.

Left to right:

Mary Wynne (Jock's sister)
Jock Findlay
Ian Findlay (Jock's son),
at the back
Lena Findlay (Jock's wife)
William Findlay (Jock's father)

Jock with his sons Leonard (left) and Ian (right)

Facing page: Sybil Cavanagh, former local history librarian West Lothian Council

SYBIL CAVANAGH grew up in Fife and is a graduate of St Andrews University. After a diploma in librarianship at the University of Wales, she worked in Wigan and then Glasgow, where a longstanding interest in Scottish history developed into a particular interest in local history. She was for 26 years the local history librarian for West Lothian, and built up a comprehensive library of books, photos, maps and other information on the county, now housed in Linlithgow Partnership Centre. Since her retirement in 2016, she has continued her research into West Lothian's history, with a particular interest in the 18th and early 19th centuries, and West Lothian's links with the slave trade. She has published books on the history of Blackburn, Pumpherston, Bathgate and Whitburn.

Sybil Cavanagh

NEIL FINDLAY was born in Bangour hospital and lives in Fauld-house. Like his father and great-grandfather before him, he served an apprenticeship as a bricklayer and for ten years worked as a tradesman alongside his Da, Ian. He attended evening classes at West Lothian College before graduating from Strathclyde and Glasgow Universities. He worked in the social housing sector and was a secondary school teacher for ten years. In 2003, he was elected onto West Lothian Council as a councillor for the Breich Valley ward before being elected in 2011 to the Scottish Parliament as an MSP for the Lothian region. He is standing down from parliament at the 2021 election.

Neil is married to Fiona and they have a grown-up daughter, Chloe. Neil has written many articles for newspapers and magazines and has previously published a book *Socialism and Hope: A Journey Through Turbulent Times.*

Neil Findlay MSP

Note: 'The Raws' is a reference to the rows ('raws' in Scots) of cottage style houses that were generally of a uniform construction with common gable ends, built by the Pumpherston Oil Company to house shale miners and those who worked in the industry.

Typical shale miners' raws at Addiewell

The South Village Pumpherston raws today

Lamp oil wagon (Almond Valley Heritage Trust)

Scottish Shale Oil Industry Timeline

Before 1850
The only oils available to fuel lamps or lubricate machinery were made from plants or animals. These oils were smelly and expensive.

1850
James 'Paraffin' Young created a process to produce oil from a special type of coal. They began to build the world's first mineral oil works at Boghead near Bathgate. He had a patent on this process meaning only he was allowed to use it to get the oil from the special types of coal.

During the 1850s
James Young developed a fuel for oil lamps which he called 'paraffine'. This new fuel was an immediate success. The process is used throughout the world and James 'Paraffin' Young became rich and famous. James Young had a patent on this fuel meaning only he could use the process unless someone had paid him a licence fee.

1859
The world's first oil well is drilled in the USA providing a much simpler and cheaper way of producing mineral oil. American oil is soon being imported into Britain.

1862
James Young's patents run out sparking 'oilmania'. Throughout the Scottish coalfields people try to get rich quick by opening their own oilworks. Most only last a few years.

Miner's tally token from Pumpherston Oil Company
(Almond Valley Heritage Trust)

1866
James Young begins construction of a huge oilworks at Addiewell which uses oil-shale instead of coal.

1870
James Young sells his interest in Young's Paraffin Light and Mineral Oil Company, and retires to enjoy his fortune.

1877
The Broxburn Oil Company is established, using a new design of shale retort. The success of this new company encourages others to open large scale oil works.

1885
The invention of the motor car.

1894
The Pumpherston Oil Company invents an even better shale retort. The company grows quickly to become the most successful of the Scottish oil companies.

1901
Queen Victoria dies.

1905–1910
A time of success and richness for the five major shale oil companies. Oil works are made bigger and improved, but

Shale miner's helmet
(Almond Valley Heritage Trust)

the Scottish companies continue to compete against each other instead of joining together to combat the threat of the American Oil import.

1914
First World War declared.

1917
The Russian Revolution.

1918
End of the First World War.

1919
The shale oil industry is unable to compete against cheap imported oils. The Scottish companies join together to form Scottish Oils Ltd, part of a government group that became BP.

1922
Scottish Oils open the Grangemouth refinery to process imported crude oil. The skills and experience of the shale oil companies was vital in the development of the new international oil company.

1925
A public enquiry concludes that shale oil will never again be able to compete with cheaper imported fuels. Oilworks close

Shale miner's lamp
(Almond Valley Heritage Trust)

with terrible consequences to the thousands employed by the industry. The General Strike takes place.

1927
The Jazz Singer, the first movie with sound released.

1928
Women win the same voting rights as men in the UK.

1931
The government reduces tax on Scottish oil to prevent the total closure of the shale oil industry.

1939
Second World War declared.

1941
New shale mines are opened and a major new oilworks is built so that Britain would not be so dependent on imported oils in the event of war.

1945
Second World War ends.

During the 1950s the tax advantage of shale oil is gradually reduced. Oilworks and mines close.

Shale miner's pickaxe
(Almond Valley Heritage Trust)

1962
The last Scottish shale oil works is closed.

1969
Man lands on the moon.

1971
The first email sent.

1993
The Pumpherston BP detergent works closed.

1999
Scottish Parliament reconvened for the first time since 1707.

2001
Terror attacks on the World Trade Centre in New York.

2008
Barack Obama is first black president elected in the US.

2014
Referendum on Scottish independence.

Pumpherston Oil Works with the shale bings
(Almond Valley Heritage Trust)

Pumpherston and the Shale Industry:

A Concise Overview

Sybil Cavanagh

PUMPHERSTON VILLAGE WAS built by the Pumpherston Oil Company in 1884 to house those coming to work in its new shale mines and oil works. The company was joining an industry established over 30 years earlier by James Young. He was the first to produce oil from minerals on a commercial scale, opening his works at Bathgate in 1851 to process the cannel coal of Boghead. When the Boghead coal began to run out, he turned his attention to shale, the plentiful mineral that underlay large parts of West Lothian.

When Young's protective patents ran out, some 43 works were set up in the Almond Valley of West Lothian alone to cash in on the new industry. But poor trade conditions and competition from America quickly put many of the smaller companies out of business; by 1877 only seven works remained. Among them was the Uphall Mineral Oil Company, set up by Pumpherston estate's owner Peter McLagan MP and his partners. They had established oil works at Uphall Station in the 1870s, and built Stankards Rows (the Randy Raws) just north of the station to house the workers.

Renewed prosperity in the early 1880s led to the setting up of more than a dozen new companies, including Pumpherston's in late 1883. William Fraser (30), manager of Uphall Mineral Oil Company, with his brother Archibald, leased the mineral rights on the Pumpherston estate from Peter McLagan MP and in 1883–84 began to build the Pumpherston Oil Works. Within a year, the works were in operation; and within ten years, the works covered 23 acres and employed 700 men. It proved to be one of the most successful companies, due to good technical and financial management, and generally good industrial relations with an experienced and stable workforce. The Pumpherston company was large enough to withstand temporary downturns in the economy, increased competition from rival local companies and from foreign oil and it took over failed companies at Seafield, Deans and Tarbrax.

Just before the First World War, five large companies remained: Young's, Oakbank's, Broxburn's, Philpstoun's and the Pumpherston Oil Company. Their output of shale had grown enormously since the 1880s, their efficiency had increased, yet their share of UK oil consumption had dropped from 40 per cent to 14 per cent, dwarfed by imported oils. The shale industry had reached its heyday, employing some 12,000 men just before the First World War. But from then on, it would be a story of decline.

Technical & working conditions

Pumpherston Oil Company sank six shale mines around the village and built a crude oil works, a refinery and railway lines to take its products to market. Unlike American crude oil which gushed out of the ground, Scottish shale had to be mined, crushed and retorted (heated to a high temperature and then distilled). The resulting crude oil then had to be refined by further distillation and chemical treatments to produce the sellable end products: lubricating oil, paraffin and motor spirit. The wax removed from the paraffin was sold for candlemaking and sulphate of ammonia was yet another valuable by-product, used as a fertiliser.

Pumpherston's works was built when the simple early technology of shale processing had grown more complex and more efficient. Competition forced the shale companies to ever greater technical efficiency and higher output but, despite these achievements, it was only the lower duty levied by the government on home-produced oil that allowed them to compete with foreign imports.

Working conditions for the workers were poor and dangerous: there were falls of shale or stone from the roof, accidents from misfired shots, explosions, runaway hutches, scalds and burns, entanglement in machinery, falls from a height or down the shafts. A boiler explosion in 1890 mangled and killed three men. In the years between 1895 and 1911, 23 employees of the Pumpherston Oil Company were killed in work accidents. Legislation ensured that conditions gradually improved, but shale works and mines could never be a safe or pleasant working environment.

Decline and fall

In 1919, at the end of the First World War, the five surviving shale companies (including Pumpherston) amalgamated under the name Scottish Oils Ltd (SOL), and became part of the Anglo-Persian Oil Company. This reorganisation resulted in greater efficiencies and improved marketing. William Fraser Jnr of Pumpherston, who during the First World War had worked closely with the government to maximise shale oil output, became SOL's first managing director.

In 1919 James Bryson was appointed Pumpherston Works' manager, and by means of the efficient retort which he designed, reduced the cost of shale mining at Pumpherston by a significant amount. In the 1920s, SOL began to refine crude oil supplied by the Anglo-Persian Oil Company. Landed at Grangemouth, the oil was brought to Uphall by pipeline, and a refinery was built at Grangemouth in 1924 to refine it. Grangemouth was chosen by Anglo-Persian in order to be close to the expertise of West Lothian's shale industry.

SOL tried hard to promote Scottish shale during the difficulties and recessions of the 1920s and 1930s, but it was a hard time for the industry, and still harder for the workmen and their families. A contract to supply shale oil to the Admiralty was lost in 1925, and that same year Pumpherston's crude oil works closed as was No.4 mine, the last of the six mines around the village. Cuts to wages were imposed followed by strikes and hardship. In 1932–33, SOL introduced the 'spread-over' scheme whereby employees worked three weeks out of four in order to share out the available work and avoid redundancies. But, by 1938, the amount of shale being processed each year was only half that of 1924, and the workforce too had halved. It was only the Second World War with its renewed demand for oil that brought a measure of prosperity to the industry again.

After the war, the unequal struggle resumed, with the Scottish shale industry continuing to try and compete with the vast quantities of available foreign oils; the decline of the industry was all too evident to its management and workers alike. SOL struggled on for another couple of decades, and continued to improve efficiency by recycling spent shale into SOL bricks at Pumpherston works, refining crude oil from wells in

Lancashire and Nottinghamshire and setting up a detergent works to produce liquid detergent from shale oil, marketed under the name Iranopol and later By-Prox. The brickworks and detergent works gave employment to large numbers of women.

In 1928 the government had imposed a duty on imported oils, but exempted Scottish shale oil. This was what enabled SOL to keep in competition with imported oils – the 'preference' making up half the company's profits in the 1950s. When Britain joined the European Free Trade Association (a forerunner of the EU) in 1962 it obliged the government to withdraw the preference. The industry, with one fell swoop, became uncompetitive, and in April 1962 was suddenly and brutally closed down. For a couple of years, Pumpherston Refinery continued to refine English oil, and the detergent works carried on, using Welsh oil, until final closure in 1993 – the end of 100 years of the shale industry in Pumpherston.

Living in the village

The building of the village was begun in 1884 at the same time as the works so that there would be no delay in bringing in workers. First came the Works Rows in Drumshoreland Road, then the Auld Rows (North Village) and the New Rows (South Village). The standard of the housing was relatively good for the times in order to secure 'superior workmen'. Most were single ends or two-roomed houses, which were improved *c*. 1900–14 with the addition of porches containing a sink and a WC. However, even by the standards of the time, the houses were overcrowded, with over three persons per room; mining families tended to be large. Some 44 per cent of households also included lodgers.

In the first seven years of the village, some 1,400 people came to Pumpherston to work in the new mines and works. One third came from elsewhere in West Lothian or Midlothian (probably already with experience in the shale industry or mining), and another third came from Ireland. It was a company village: of the 483 working-age males in 1891, at least 469 worked in the Pumpherston mines and works. Only those working for the company were eligible for a company house, and of the 224 houses in the village 209 were owned by the Oil Company and 15 by West Calder Co-op.

Pumpherston Oil Company (POC) was noted for providing good facilities for its workforce – a school in 1886 and Institute Hall in 1891 – and financial help to a variety of local sports and social organisations. However, it took a firm stance on alcohol, and refused the use of any land or property for a pub. The village remained dry until the local football and bowling clubs set up licensed social clubs in the 1950s and 1960s.

The company provided a store, but did not try to prevent the arrival of other shops. West Calder Co-op opened a large branch in 1887 and a large extension in 1925, providing a range of departments. The Co-op's employees were not entitled to a POC house, so the Co-op built some 20 houses at Society Place.

Jock Findlay's reminiscences provide a wonderful insight into everyday life in the Raws – the closeness of the community, the sense of security experienced through growing up in a small village in which everyone knew everyone else. There was plenty to do – schooldays, leisure and sports activities organised or subsidised by the company, playing in the fields and burns – in some ways an idyllic rural childhood. The difficulties of making ends meet seldom touch children; it's the parents who do the worrying, but there were certainly times when lack of work and lack of money made life hard.

It was a self-sufficient village in many ways – people worked, lived, shopped and socialised there. But they were bound to the village by the paternalism of the company: it provided decent housing and good facilities in return for hard work and abiding by the rules. The restrictions were relatively minor – not being allowed to choose the paint colour of your front door, or get a drink locally or having to keep your garden tidy; and a reprimand from the manager if you stepped out of line. But if a man wanted to oppose company policy, or to work elsewhere, he had to give up not just his safe job, but also his house, his friends and community, and move away from the village. However benign its intentions, the company exercised a powerful hold over its employees, which was loosened only by the availability of council houses from the late 1930s onwards.

Jock Findlay's book is not a rose-tinted view of the past – it acknowledges the hardships, inequalities and paternalism. If there is nostalgia, it is not so much for the hardness of the life and the work, but for the community and the ethos – care for one another, and care for surroundings that were enjoyed in common. It is a glimpse of a world which set a high value on the ability to do hard, skilled manual work, on thrifty independence, decency and self-respect. It was a world of shared dangers, shared pleasures: a communal, sociable way of life that has almost disappeared.

Neil Findlay with the plywood bath panel that has Jock's abbreviated life story on the rear

Discovering Jock's Journal

Neil Findlay

AT THE TIME of the Scottish independence referendum, I was canvassing in the South Village area of Pumpherston where my Granda Jock was brought up and where he and my Granny Lena lived out their lives until they passed away in 1999 and 2005 respectively.

Pumpherston, a shale oil village dominated by the Pumpherston Oil Company, was central to the birth of the first oil boom of James 'Paraffin' Young. 'The works' as it was known went on to be owned and run by British Petroleum, or BP, right into the 1990s, when my uncle Leonard – my Da's twin brother and Jock and Lena's son – was the Chief Electrician and the last person out before the doors were closed forever.

During that canvass session, I knocked the door of my Granny's old house at 214 South Village and got speaking to Mrs Edwards and her husband, the couple who live in the house now and who had bought it when my Granny went into sheltered housing in East Calder a decade before. She told me that every time they redecorated the house, they found stories, jokes and poems written by my Granda on the plastered walls below the old wallpaper. In the middle of telling me this, Mrs Edwards disappeared back into the house and returned with a two-by-two foot board of plywood, which had been the end panel of the bath that was in the house. When Mr Edwards removed the panel to replace it with a modern one, he found that Jock had written a summary of his life story

Oakbank Village in the early 1900s (Almond Valley Heritage Trust).

on the other side. It had been hidden away in the darkness for many years. It was amazing to see this discovery and read his story. Mrs Edwards insisted on giving me the board, which I now have in my house. I have to admit my Mum and I shed a tear reading it for the first time. It is something I will always treasure.

Jock was a plumber and lead burner; he was a very skilled craftsman and was as meticulous in his appearance as he was with his trade and all the handywork he did around the

house and garden. He married my Granny Lena, who came from the village of Oakbank and was adopted as a child. She worked as a domestic servant before going on to run the Pumpherston village general store with Jock's sister Mary, who my Da called 'the Queen'. Mary was very much a lady but with a great sense of fun and an infectious laugh.

Following the discovery of the board, I searched for and found a small hardback book that was the one personal effect I got when Lena and Jock died. When I dug out this small journal,

I felt compelled to transcribe it and see if it could be made into a book, putting on permanent record Jock's personal account of life in Pumpherston – in his day, a very important industrial village in east-central Scotland.

It is the record of the life and experience of Jock Findlay, a proud, good, clever working-class man. It tells of school, work, family life; of the community and the culture and ways of a bygone era; of a time of hard work, thrift, decency and respect – but it also tells about struggle, hardship and poverty.

It dates from Jock's earliest memories, around 1919 – ending as his eyesight deteriorated and he could no longer see to write anymore, around 1994. *Life in the Raws* is reproduced here just as Jock wrote it, with minimal change or input from me.

A picture of Oakbank has been used as the cover image of this book because it was the most evocative picture I could find from the times of the shale boom. To me it captures the architecture of the raws and the people who inhabited them in one powerful image.

> *Neil Findlay,*
> *MSP for the Lothian Region*

Life in the Raws:
Memories of a Shale Oil Village

Jock Findlay

Miner working a shale seam
(Almond Valley Heritage Trust)

THE VILLAGE OF Pumpherston grew and developed around the shale oil works. 'The Work' was founded in 1884 on the east side of the village by the Pumpherston Oil company. The oil (pronounced 'ile') works and the shale mines that were scattered throughout the area were the main source of employment. There were eight shale mines that I can recollect, most to east of the village except the No.4 mine that lay to the north.

The shale was transported from the mines to the breakers (crushers) by hutches or bogies that were hauled along rails on a wire towrope that ran on continuous loop. The laden hutches were tipped into the breaker, which crushed the shale into small pieces before it was burned in large brick retorts. The gas produced in this process was then condensed into crude oil. This was refined to produce various oil-based products such as paraffin, lubricating oil, diesel and light and heavy burning oil. Coke was produced for furnaces, wax for candles and dousy for miner's lamps. The process also produced sulphate of ammonia, which for many years was exported to China for use in the rice fields.

Row after row of large iron stills (pots) stood, encased in brickwork fired underneath by a furnace to boil the oil. Twenty-foot-high tanks stood on brickwork buttresses into which green and blue oil was pumped. This oil was washed with caustic soda and sulphuric acid. It was then separated with the tarry residue left behind after the liquid was run off by gravity. The residue left behind was burned in still fires.

The burnt shale from the retorts was tipped around the refinery in vast pink bings rising to around 500 feet in some places, covering vast areas of countryside – these can still be

A shale miner filling the hutches
(Almond Valley Heritage Trust)

seen in Pumpherston, Broxburn (where the tip resembles Ayers Rock), Winchburgh and of course the famous Five Sisters Bings near Polbeth and West Calder, now a listed industrial monument. The MP Tam Dalyell fought to have these bings recognised for their industrial importance and a key part of the communities' heritage.

The tip men were mainly Irishmen and they experienced many a rough and stormy night working on top of the 'pink mountains'. There were no lights at the tip face and the hutches had to be coupled in pitch darkness. The wind and rain drove from the south-west as they uncoupled the hutches, each weighing around one tonne, and manually pushed them the 120 yards from the tower to the tipping area.

Winter conditions were desperate, every day they would be wet and frozen to the bone but on summer days, they had the benefit of magnificent views across the county, towards Edinburgh and along the Fife coast. From the top they could see the network of vast shale bings that stretched throughout east-central Scotland – from the Chippings at Penicuik outside Edinburgh to Burntisland in Fife.

As I write (1980), I have watched for the last 30 years the Roman Camp Tip having shale taken from it for the building trade – they are still nowhere near half way through.

The vastness of these man-made mountains can be gauged when you consider that in 1960 the Dean Tip was estimated to contain 22 million tonnes of spent shale, not to mention the many thousands of tonnes that would have been spread across the countryside by the elements. Every ounce of this material had been retrieved from the bowels of the earth by the only

Pumpherston Oil Works (Almond Valley Heritage Trust)

means available at that time – pick, shovel and man's bare hands – an extraordinary human effort when you think of it.

There is no doubt in my mind these tips are a monument to the men who contributed to their creation. As the former shale workers die off so the bings will shrink through erosion. Soon neither will remain.

There were three tips belonging to the Pumpherston Oil Company, the Old Rows tip, the Mair Road tip and the No. 5 mine tip.

In 1929 wages at the work were as follows: 36 shillings a week for a labourer and 50 shillings for a tradesman. My wage when I started in the plumbers shop was 11 shillings and fourpence. The working day was 6.20am until 9.00am, breakfast from

A Pumpherston Oil Company tanker (Almond Valley Heritage Trust)

9.00am until 9.40 am. Then work again until dinner, from 1.00pm to 1.30pm, finishing at 4.00pm. You worked these hours Monday to Friday and until 1.00pm on a Saturday. All in all a 48 hour week. Wages were paid on a Friday.

The oil company owned most of the houses in the village apart from around 24 that were owned by the Co-op and ten that were privately owned and rented out. Renting a house from the work cost 1 shilling and sixpence a week for a two-room house and 1 shilling per week for a one room house.

An example of a plumber's wages (Almond Valley Heritage Trust)

The work was run by the manager director Mr Bryson. Not only did he run the oil works, he ran the entire village and did so with a rod of iron. If you stepped out of line then you could safely bet that the following day your father would be called into the works' office to account for your actions. And God help any man who came home drunk on a Saturday night and disturbed the peace of the village. This type of behaviour would result in a severe reprimand at the works' office on the Monday morning.

The Works manager, Mr James Bryson
(Almond Valley Heritage Trust)

Obituary, *The Scotsman*, Monday 20 January 1930

The death took place last night at his residence at Ballengeich, Pumpherston, Mid Calder, of Mr James Bryson, in his 77th year. He was general works manager of the Scottish Oils (Ltd.) and a director of the Company. Mr Bryson served on the Parish School Board for many years, and up to the time of his death was a member of Midlothian County Council and the Lothians War Pensions Committee, on both of which he did excellent work. He was a devoted Churchman, and a generous donor to Bridgend u.f. Church, Mid Calder.

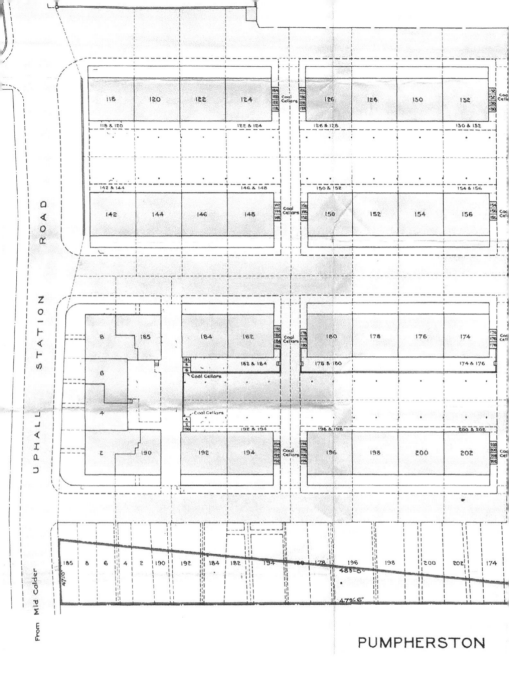

Plan of South Village where Jock and Lena lived in their later years

44

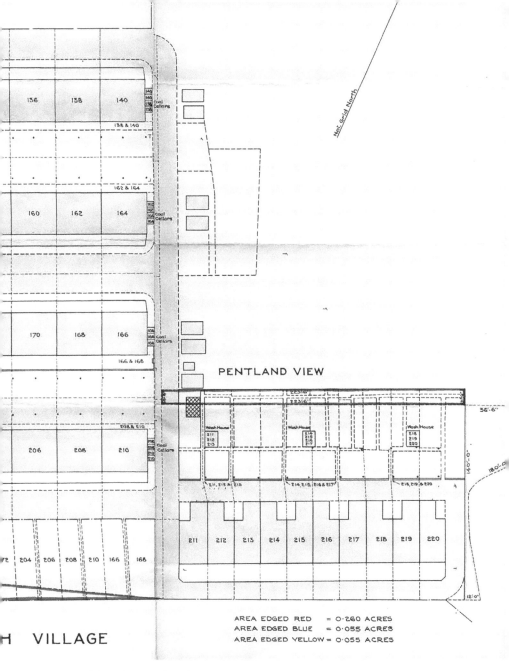

PENTLAND VIEW

H VILLAGE

AREA EDGED RED   = 0·260 ACRES
AREA EDGED BLUE   = 0·055 ACRES
AREA EDGED YELLOW = 0·055 ACRES

(Almond Valley Heritage Trust)

45

Overall, life in the village was peaceful with none of the vandalism that has come to be the accepted way of life today. When the dark nights came, there were no electric lights on the street. This changed when the Co-op installed three lights – one at the school, one at the store corner and one at the north end of the village. It was not until 1925 that the work installed street lights throughout the village.

Around the village, there is some lovely woodland. The Store Wood, the Thicket Wood, the Heather Row Wood, the Pew Road Wood, the Scots Wood, the Soldier's Wood, the Clay Road Wood and Craw Flee Wood. These were the playground of many children in the village. I remember as a boy finding some old stone-lined wells at the south end of the Scots wood, which runs along the south of the village. Who used these wells or what their purpose was no one knows but it seems as if they must have supplied the village or a previous settlement sometime in the past.

The ponds were kept clean and were home to numerous swans who made their nests there every year, rearing a brood of young. There were thousands of frogs that bred in the ponds and each year we kept tadpoles in glass jam jars, watching in wonder the amazing change from tadpole to frog. This is where we learned biology and all about the natural world on our doorstep. There were four ponds – the Cooler Pond, the Works Pond, the New Rows Pond, the Millers Pond. Only the Works Pond survives today (1980) but it is nothing like the pond we knew as children.

On the outskirts of the village there used to be a stable for the horse that pulled the bucket cart for the 'scaffy'. That was the

The view today from Craigshill up over the farmland to South Village Pumpherston

name we gave the street sweepers in those days. The horse's name was Bobby and he had only one eye. He always stopped at certain houses and refused to go another step until he was given a slice of bread from the woman who usually gave him his breakfast piece. The scaffy's name was Cockie Flucker. He kept the village really clean by sweeping the sheugh and cleaning the sewers and woe betide anyone he saw throwing a piece of paper on the street. If you were at the bottom of the street and he was at the other end you would hear the roars of him and see him brandishing his brush to such an extent that we were glad to put the paper in the bucket to quieten him down and stave off his attack.

Daniel Miller farmed Pumpherston Farm at that time. He was a good farmer and worked the ground well. The methods used were very different from now, most noticeably there were no tractors to pull the plough. Miller's plough was pulled by a pair of horses guided by the plough share. It took a long time to plough a large field but it was sight to behold watching these large beautiful Clydesdale horses straining at the plough and seeing the skilled ploughman working them across the field. Before the war, a farm would employ as many as ten men but following the introduction of the tractor a good-sized farm could be worked with two or three men.

Where the new town of Livingston now stands there used to be at least 20 farms. And this was prime farming land, now confiscated for housing. You could walk the fields of Pumpherston Farm and the farmer knew there would be no damage, indeed he provided stiles to assist people over his fences.

Sundays were a big family day – I had to have my suit and best clothes on and shiny shoes to wear. As a family, we always walked on a Sunday usually along the banks of the River Almond and the 'feeder' burn that ran into it. We would then walk home along the railway line that went from Uphall to East Calder.

In the summer, these days were marvellous and usually really warm and the sun shone for weeks on end. There was the lovely scent of clover, honeysuckle and many other kinds of wild flowers. There was the humming of bees and the songs of birds.

Sundays were peaceful days for the village. I was told by my parents not to whistle or play the gramophone. When I

Leonard and Ian in their Sunday best

returned from my walk I was stripped of my best clothes and spent the rest of the day at home. Our family were not great church people and damned few in village were as far as I was can remember. The villagers were more manager-fearing than God-fearing!

Around 1921 (at least I think that was the year) the oil works went on strike. I can remember the coal miners were on strike at the same time and following this there were lock outs in 1924 and the general strike in 1926.

These were extremely tough times for the working class. I remember the coal miners parading through the village in fancy dress following the pipe and brass bands. Each miner held a collecting can to try to raise funds for what we called soup kitchens. The money was given to the women of the village who would buy ingredients for soup and loaves of bread to feed the children and families of the men on strike.

49

West Calder and Addiewell women protesting against the withholding of parish payments to families of striking miners (Almond Valley Heritage Trust)

The Pumpherston soup kitchen was in the school and was used mainly by larger families, some of whom had up to 12 children. These big families were raised in room and kitchen houses with only three bed recesses. There was no such thing as bathrooms or central heating. In those days the only heat came from the open fire and on this all cooking was done. There must have been some problems in these packed households. If we were in need of a bath we went to the wooden washhouse at the rear of the house and filled the bathtub from the wash boiler after the clothes washing was finished.

When it was washday four tenants shared the washhouse. Each tenant had their allocated washday. My mother used to do washing for the local farm owner and the labourers at the work and was paid two and six a week – today's equivalent of 15 pence! There were no washing machines, of course, all of the clothes had to be scrubbed on a wash board with metal ribs. The washing was rubbed up and down the metal ribs to loosen the dirt. Washday usually started at 5.00am with the light of fire under the boiler helping the women to see what they were doing. The well-stoked fire meant hot water was available all day.

The gardens in the village were a treat to see. Every householder had to care for their garden and it was their job to ensure they were properly attended to. Almost all grew their own vegetables. Some of the miners also had allotments, which were situated between the Raws and the 'Magazine' – so called because it held the powder for blasting the shale.

For entertainment, we had the children's Band of Hope, which met once a week in the Institute Hall. This was a kind of religious gathering for children and every three months we had a soirée with tea and buns which was a big event for the children. They were always a guaranteed full house for that. Then there was the Kinderspiel held by the choir and some very good plays were performed by them.

I remember going with my elder brother to see *Rob Roy*. There was a crowd of boys around my brother's age and it was really something for me to mix with them. Well every one of them was keen to see Rob Roy being shot and this scene was keenly anticipated. To see and hear a real gun make a loud bang as it went off was very exciting. As their expectations reached its height, I announced I needed the toilet. Amid whispers of 'Let him pish on the flair,' and 'Can he no haud it in?', I was unceremoniously yanked out of my seat and shoved to the door, when lo and behold the gun went off with the loudest bang I have ever heard. Believe you me I wished then it had been real AND aimed at me.

Given that clothes were in short supply, families did everything to make them last. When you tore the arse out of them sliding down bings or climbing on a tree in the wood they were neatly patched and ready for a new day. I say neatly patched, because even though it usually was a different material being used my mother took great pride in her needlework. Having a patch was better than having your arse bare to the world and the cauld wind.

Very few children had school coats and our 'uniform' was a jersey with two buttons at the neck, a shirt and a tied semmit (singlet). Short flannel trousers, knitted socks and heavy boots with rows of tacketts or nails finished off the outfit. The 'tacketty boots' never seemed to fit properly and were agony when suffering from chilblains in winter but as there was nowt else – you had to make do and suffer. I used to try and hold hot cloths to the leather to see if it would stretch before leaving for school in the morning.

There was no such luxury as school dinners or milk for the children then. We had to run home for our piece of jam or cheese. The children of farm workers used to carry their two pieces with them, usually butter sprinkled with sugar. They would also bring a flask of cold tea which could be heated on the classroom fire in winter but they had to drink it cold in summer as the fire was left unlit in the warmer months.

In recent years, there has been great controversy about the use of the belt for punishment in our schools. In my day, it was used freely and few parents objected when it was. In lessons we were told to sit with our arms folded in front of us and if you unfolded them you received the belt or if you were lucky you got a bloody good telling off from the teacher. If you got the belt and teacher misjudged the distance to your hands you ended up with great red weals on your wrists.

From time to time teachers were issued with new Lochgelly tawse belts. I have no idea why, because even with regular use in our school they never appeared to deteriorate. Some of the teachers had a real glint in their eye as they showed the class their new weapon and its capabilities.

School was also a place of fun and we had some great laughs. I remember we had a young teacher who the headmaster was very fond of. She would often be called by him and spend a whole hour in his anteroom. We all knew what was going on and during this time the classroom would descend into a riot. It was pleasure all round for class, teacher and head teacher.

One day the headteacher sent a boy to the bank in Mid Calder on an errand. The boy was picked because he was the only one to come to school by bicycle, a very rare possession back then. The boy set off but a few minutes into his journey forgot what he was going for and had to return to the headmaster's room. Lo and behold the heidy and the young teacher were at it full pelt on his big desk – red faces all round and much shouting ensued but no belt was used – must have been the heidy's guilt at getting caught.

The class used to do hand work (crafts). We made mats and picture frames from raffia, there was always lots of strands of the stuff lying on the floor. On the pretence of gathering up the loose strands the boys used to look up the teacher's skirt and pass round to each other the colour of her bloomers. This caused great hilarity until one day when one of the boys was on his knees checking out today's colour the teacher stepped back and almost fell over him. There was almost a murder in the classroom with fists and belt used to deliver the punishment. That put an end to our bloomer watch game – well, for a few weeks at least.

On a Saturday morning, before the refinery closed at 1.00pm, I was sent to collect a five-gallon drum of paraffin oil. It was a hard job for an eight- or nine-year-old to pull this home on a home-made wheelbarrow, which had iron wheels that didn't run smoothly on a dirt track, especially in the wet. If I remember right the five gallons cost 1 shilling and sixpence.

Every week an Italian man called Angelo wheeled another type of wooden barrow like a miniature farm cart, this time with wooden wheels which were iron shod. On the barrow he had

School and Institute Hall (Almond Valley Heritage Trust)

a handmade sink container, kept cool by sawdust. This kept the ice cream from melting. He pushed that heavy barrow up and down the braes between Mid Calder, Pumpherston, East Calder, Oakbank and all the way over to Broxburn all for a few pennies profit. A cornet cost a ha'penny, it was a penny for a slider (two wafers with ice cream in between) and a penny ha'penny for two sponge biscuits with ice cream. When I think of him now and the physical graft and effort he put into making a living to bring up his family, it is nothing short of a miracle. But then no one really gave it a thought – everyone had to work bloody hard just to get by.

On Saturdays, the pictures would come to the village. We had cinema at night but also a morning showing which we called the 'day bells' When we heard the old van chugging up the quarry brae the older boys would try to jump on the running board to be first to get the hand bills (advertising flyers) to deliver round the doors. These showed that day's big movies. They would get a free pass for their efforts.

In the village, an old Irishwoman, Biddy Smith, had been allowed to have a shop in her house. An old dresser served as the counter. In the winter she lit an oil lamp in the window to let people know she was open and show off the toffees, sweets and other goodies that we could only dream of buying.

The village had many characters. For one, there was Jock 'Brick' Maywood – the only nice thing about Jock was his second name. He was not worthy of the images a 'Maywood' conjures up. Every Saturday the work finished at 12 noon. Jock always went to Edinburgh after he finished and returned late. His wife always nagged him wanting to know where he was and what he was doing in 'the toon'. One Saturday he agreed to take her along and walked her around Edinburgh all day until the last train had gone, meaning they had to walk the 12 miles home. As Mrs Maywood was a very stout woman, this must have been a big ordeal for her.

Next door to the Maywoods lived Squabbles Martin. Squabbles had been, much to Brick Maywood's ire (he wasn't offered an extra shift), asked to do a Sunday shift. There was no such thing as alarm clocks to wake people for work, we all just seemed to wake on time. To try and get one back on Squabbles, Brick lifted the rag rug from the hearth and hung it over Squabbles' window. Of course, when he woke

A Pumpherston Oil Company steam engine (Almond Valley Heritage Trust)

he thought it was dark and went back to sleep, missing his Sunday shift – never to be asked again.

On the other side of the Maywoods lived the McGinty family. Their son Eddie was a chancer and a bit of a comic. He was also his own worst enemy, having been drummed out of the Scots Guards (I never knew anyone else at that time ever having suffered that fate).

There used to be a railway line between Uphall Station and the camps at East Calder. It was used to infill the old limestone quarries with all the refuse from Edinburgh. The line crossed the Almond Valley viaduct. The walk down that way in the summer was lovely. Anyhow, Eddie's parents were going away for the weekend and had taken the two youngest boys with them. The mother warned Eddie before she went to 'remember and get up for work in the morning'. These were the days when the bed was in a recess in the wall and to get privacy you pulled the curtains over when you went to sleep. On returning home on the Sunday night, Mr and Mrs McGinty found the curtains closed. On pulling them open, Eddie woke with a start and asked, 'Did you miss the bus?' He had slept for almost 36 hours.

Another of the village's characters was an alcoholic called Peely. Everyone knew him and he took great delight in leading the pipe band around the village on special occasions. He had been a drummer in the band years ago before the drink got a hold of him. On one occasion he was leading the parade in Mid Calder with his chest stuck out strutting like a bantam cock. When the procession went to take the West Calder road Peely marched straight on for city yards before realising what had happened – it was hilarious.

Willie McDill was one of our neighbours. On one occasion he took unwell and had to be admitted to Bangour Hospital. When he was discharged my wife Lena asked him if he 'was feeling better now?'

'Aye,' said Willie, 'but when I got home I couldnae stop counting my money. I just couldnae stop. I was really puzzled until the doactor telt me he had given me a transfusion using the Mid Calder bank manager's blood!'

The village and the work was blessed with some great men

and women – great worthies and every time their call came it saddened me more.

Funerals were a big occasion and something to be seen, the likes of which won't be seen in this day. A death in the village was an awesome occasion and affected everything not just close family and pals. In the street where the deceased lived, every house closed the curtains or blinds or blocked off the windows in some way. The hearse that carried the coffin was a four-wheeled vehicle with glass sides which was beautifully etched with vases of flowers and cherubs. At each corner a black carved vase stood. The driver wore a black top hat (we called them lum hats because they looked like the work chimney or lum). He sat on a high seat at the front of the carriage, shiny buttons on his heavy black coat and knees covered with a black 'hap' or tarpaulin. The horses were a very pure, black breed and had great plumes on their heads, the haps came right down to their hooves. Behind the hearse was the cab which held four of the nearest relatives of the deceased, then another cab holding the next nearest relatives and so on.

Women never went to the graveyard in those days, a shame I always thought as this was the last opportunity with their loved ones. The men who paid their respects at the graveside walked to the cemetery – four, five or six abreast. As the procession passed along the way men stopped and doffed their caps and lowered their heads in respect. The members of the bereaved family usually wore a black band or ribbon on the arm of their coat or jacket.

I always have an imprint in my mind of my father getting dressed for a funeral and saying to me, 'Jock, put this damned stud in this collar for me will ye?' I must have done it a hundred times. The collars were as stiff as hardboard, made that way by my mother starching the thing as hard as it could be. We never had collars on our shirts – it was always a separate item that had to be attached with a stud at the back of the neck and one at the front. Without fail, every time you had to wear one the call went out: 'Where the hell are my collar studs?' They seemed to have a life of their own and were always being mislaid.

I can recall very clearly my early memories of my faither walking up The Raws in his lum hat, swallowtail coat, with his gold Albert chain in his waistcoat and a black umbrella with gold mountings on the handle, his black boots finely polished. He was a tall man (as we all are in our family) with a long stride, carrying himself straight up and down – he was quite an imposing and authoritative sight. The style then was to wear what we called a walrus moustache, which to me seemed to give great character to his appearance.

Jock's father William Findlay with Snowy the dog

All the Irishmen in the village wore a different outfit when they paid respects. They would wear a bowler hat and a swallowtailed coat – we found this strange and saw this (wrongly) as paying lesser respect. It was just their way.

In the middle raw of the 'new raws' in South Village lived the Hughes family. They were a very talented musical family and each member sang and played an instrument. Many a night we stood outside the room window to listen to their band and the girls singing. The band were called the Joskin Brothers and we loved to hear them play. Next door to them, Mr Rochford would sit outside on a chair on a summer evening and play his melodeon. He was very good and kept us entertained.

In those days money was very scarce so we all had to make our own entertainment and make our things last. It wasn't like now, I don't see anyone with a patch on the arse of their trousers, they just throw them away and get a new pair – I don't know if this is progress or not, people seem to waste a lot.

The highlight of the year was always the Gala Day. Everyone looked forward to it. The children talked about it all year until it came and then talked about the next year's to come! Everyone tried to look their best – new or your newest trousers, held up by a snake belt, new socks knitted by my ma and new gutties (black rubbers or plimsoles). Our hair was washed and slapped down with oil. We all had to assemble in the school playground. The refinery didn't stop until 1.00pm on a Saturday so we couldn't start before then – not even on the Gala Day – oil and profit came first always! And of course all of the Gala Day committee men worked at the work so we couldn't start without them anyway.

Each year the boys would be led by the Pumpherston pipe band and the girls by the West Calder silver band and the next year we would swap over. We paraded thought the village and people flew flags and bunting made of old rags from their houses, we marched through the grounds of the work managing director's house, in one gate across the hallowed grounds and out through the other gate. One was for tradesmen and visitors like the painter, the baker's or butcher's van, the other for himself, Mr James Bryson, and other more important visitors. The parade then followed on to the chief chemist's and the mine manager's homes and other local luminaries.

When we got back to the field the committee men came round with jugs of milk and we held out our tinnies which we had carried over our shoulders on the parade (small cans in the same shape as a mug). Every child got 'a bag' with four cakes or other goodies.

We all sat in the park munching our cakes and buns. First to go was always the apple tart – we sooked and licked the apple off the top before scoffing the crisp pastry. What a treat. The rest of the bag was quickly demolished after that. We then had to queue up and were given a sixpence – aye a bloody sixpence to ourselves – this was a small fortune to us. It was soon gone as quick as the ice cream cones from Angelo and the penny cakes of chocolate that we bought with it.

After we were fed, the races started – they were always heavily contested as the first three through the tape got prize money. We all took part in the sack race, three-legged race, pillow fights, cross country and five-a-side fitba. It was a great day. Nowadays an eight-year-auld could spend a fiver a week and no be happy – we had a ball for a fraction of that.

When the school year started eftir the summer all boys were taken to Mid Calder to Jock Walker's barber's shop – his real name was Alec but everybody had another name then. Jock was a well-known local Conservative. His shop was at the back of the tobacconist shop and we used to sit in a

The store or the co-op, Pumpherston (Almond Valley Heritage Trust)

row – wee-est first. And of course we would all be giggling and kicking and nudging each other to make the next person laugh. Jock would be lathering a customer with soap prior to shaving him with an open razor. The razor having just been sharpened and finely prepared on a leather belt. Had he been distracted it would have been easy for him to draw blood from his client. So Jock would frown and cluck his tongue and tell us to be quiet.

On this particular day he roared at us to keep quiet – one of our lot bravely or stupidly said: 'It wisnae us.' Immediately we all got flung out of the shop and made to stand in the cauld and come in one at the time for 'oor thrupenny scalping' and a long lecture about our conduct before being fired back out into the cauld again. But as we trooped in and out we passed a basket full of clay pipes so we helped ourselves to a few each on the way out – we blew soapy bubbles out of them for weeks after that. We never had scented soap to wash ourselves, always soda soap and if you got it in your mouth it tastes terrible. Jock eventually moved his shop to Broxburn and one dark night he was cycling hame down Harrysmuir Road with only the carbide bicycle lamp on. As he passed someone (it would never have been me!) shouted, 'Toot, toot Tory oot, toot, toot Tory oot!' And back came a reply I still laugh at nearly 60 years later: 'Toot your nose up the parliamentary side of my arse!'

Most of the villagers did their shopping at the Co-operative which had a draper's, butcher's, baker's, shoemaker's, van shed and killing house for livestock – all now gone. They also owned around 16 houses – eight opposite the village hall and eight opposite the post office – it was called Society Place. When you went into the shop and ordered butcher meat, the butcher would write the order down, place it in half of a small wooden ball, screw on the other half of ball, place it in a wire cage then pull a string, the ball would make its way along one of three brass wire rails to the accounts office so it could be recorded. The process was repeated at the other end and back came your change. It was a feat of engineering!

The shoe department included boot and shoe makers and cobblers. When the shale mines were at full production the cobblers was always busy with men trying to get their working boots repaired to make them last. This was a real craft, sewing and mending the miners' boots. It required strength, skill and expertise but now it has gone the same way as the patched arse of our trousers – throw the boots away and get a new pair the minute there is a problem! That would have been unheard of in the 1920s.

I recall in our house there were two fancy shaped biscuit tins painted brightly with mountaineers climbing a mountain. They were kept on our mantelpiece for decoration. Well, years later, I saw the same tin in an Edinburgh second-hand shop, it had no lid and looked as though it had been played with for 90 minutes at Tynecastle – and they wanted £4.50 for it. When I think of some of the furniture and objects flung out of the workers' houses to make way for modern rubbish, there must be many regrets to this day.

There was a shop in the North Village owned by Mrs Scott – her husband was killed in the refinery when one of the foot-plates on the stills collapsed and he died as a result. I think this resulted in his widow being allowed to open the shop in her house.

The other shop at the north gate of the Institute was called the stall, as it was no more than a wooden hut and had been brought to the village from Rosyth following the 1914–18 war. It was initially run by Davy Armstrong but when he and his family moved to America it came into the possession of Davy Armit. Dave's faither and sister served in the shop right up until 1954. It was then sold to Michael Wynne, the husband of my sister Mary. During their time running the shop, the hut was demolished making way for a brick-built shop with a chemist next door – the first chemist shop in Pumpherston.

At the very north end of the village, the final shop was run by my cousin Tam Mabon. He had bought it from the Frame family, who had originally built it and the two adjoining houses. These families had funded the building of houses and shops by profiteering from having a place in the mine. The system worked like this: a man would have a certain section of the shale mine allocated to him; he in turn employed the miners and drawers to work that section (if he had sons or male relatives they would be employed to dig and draw the shale); the men who controlled these sections often worked just a few days a week, going in to check production and pay wages. Some clearly made good money off the backs of their relatives.

In the 1930s, there were two fatalities in the refinery [Jock Wylie and Bill Dornan]. These shocked the work and the village. First of all Jock Wylie fell from a high ladder when replacing a pipe joint between two cooler towers. I think he was in his mid-20s.

Obituary, *The Scotsman*, 15 August 1931

A young man named John Wyllie, who resided at Pumpherston, lost his life by an accident at the oil works. He was engaged at operations on a cooling tower, and stepped on to planks on a platform. One of the planks slipped, and Wyllie fell from a height of 20 feet. In his fall, his head struck a building, and he was killed on the spot.

Then Bill Dornan (who had played football for Hibs) was measuring the amount of oil in a stick tank when there was an explosion. It blew the 30 feet in diameter tank cover off and deposited it like a huge umbrella across the pipelines. It started a huge fire from which Bill had no escape – he was marooned 40 feet up on a walkway. He died from the terrible burns he suffered.

Photo of the explosion and fire at Pumpherston Oil Works in 1937 which killed William Dornan (inset) (Almond Valley Heritage Trust)

Work was hard and often dangerous. As boys in the summer we would spend our time watching the road workers operating the tarry boilers. These were integral to the process of road surfacing. Three iron boilers were mounted on heavy iron wheels with a coal fired furnace underneath to heat up the tar. This was pulled along by a steam traction engine.

For the week that work was going on, they would park up at the top of the brae. If you kept in with the workmen on the late shift, they would let us pull the wooden barrels by chain blocks and cleats. The cleats were put on the barrels at each end and the barrel filled with tar was pulled to the top of the boiler. The bung or plug was then released into the boiler through an aperture in the top of the lid. This was then replaced and the fire stoked up. We cleaned the tar from our hands with waste threads from the textile mills and some oil – no sterile or any other type or rags then (it must have been because we were too busy wearing them).

But this was great fun, the smell of hot tar, the boiler belching black reek and blathering to the workmen in their wee cabin. The method of resurfacing was to trail the boiler behind the steam engine, the tar flowed in a strip about a third of the width of the road. Then a gang of men threw shovels of gravel or whin chips over the tar. The chips were placed in small piles every 20 yards or so along the stretch to be laid. Once this was done, the steamroller would come along and roll the chips into the tar. This process has been modernised now with new machines and working methods but I am not sure the roads will last as long as they did by this method.

* * *

This year is 1985 and I have been thinking about my life and that of my family, friends and local community. I have come to the conclusion that my sister Mary (now 80) and I (70) are the only two left in South Village who were actually born here and were some of the first residents.

Looking back at my family's history, I can trace the Findlays to the Black Isle. They moved to Dalmeny during the Highland Clearances to a place called the 'Hanging Shaws' or 'Standing

Jock's grandfather (left) with Lord Carmichael – he worked on Carmichael's estate at Braidwood, Lanarkshire

Jock's grandparents, the Walkers

Stones'. My grandfather, who was a joiner, came to Mid Calder to renovate the church. He then met and married my Granny. They had two sons and one daughter. My Uncle James was a joiner too. My father was a bricklayer, as is my son Ian and his son Neil; my grandson has just started to serve his time as a brickie too. Janet, my Da's sister, married a serving soldier, Samuel Johnstone, and went to live in Ireland but died a young woman.

My faither met my mother at a place called Callans near Romano Bridge. He was working there at the time. They were married at Newlands Church. In 1908, my faither went by sailing ship to Sydney in Australia to build brick retorts for the emerging oil industry. These retorts were of the same design as the ones at the Pumpherston refinery.

There were six in our family, four sons and two daughters – Elizabeth, Mary, James, Lawrence, William, John and my cousin Thomas Mabon was brought up as our brother as his mother Elizabeth had died when he was just two. James died aged 52, Lawrence 67, William 64.

James had worked as a bus driver with Simpson's, then Allan & Kennedy, then finally with SMT at the Broxburn depot. Lawrence was a process worker at the sulphate of ammonia plant at the Pumpherston Oil Company (POC) refinery. William was a still repairer attached on to the boilermakers at the POC. I served my time as a plumber and lead burner under the old foreman, 'Pin leg Wull Broon'.

We lived at Number 140 at the foot of 'The School Raw' – the official address was 140 New Rows, Pumpherston by Mid Calder. You could always depend on the mail being delivered on time unlike now despite all the new requirements they have. Our postman was Wullie Smith. He had suffered a spinal injury in the 1914–18 war and had to wear a steel spinal support. Before the days of vans he would walk from Mid Calder to Pumpherston, bags loaded with parcels and letters making sure they were delivered on time. And did he get the full wage for his efforts? Did he hell; they deducted his war pension from his bloody wages! These are the so called Victorian values that that woman Thatcher wants us to return

On the far left of this 1908 photograph is William Findlay, Jock's father
(Almond Valley Heritage Trust)

to. When I compare then to now it's the same mob that are
in power – it's all for them and nothing for working people.

Last week my Grandson John got married, the first of the
grandchildren to wed. It was a great day with around 160
guests, all family and friends. Just after this I had a wee problem
with my ticker and I have to take the next few months a bit
easy. John is Ian's son (Leonard is my other son – Ian and he
are twins) and there is Anna and Neil.

As I said, Ian is a bricklayer and is married to Margaret, a

Back row: William Findlay and William Johnston – Jock and Lena's fathers
Middle row: Ian Findlay and Leonard Findlay Front: Liffey the greyhound

Jock and Lena

Jock and Lena preparing to leave hospital after Jock had spent a year
recuperating, following an accident where he lost his right leg

primary school teacher. My God! A schoolteacher married to a brickie! In my young day that would never have happened. The school teacher would have married another school teacher or a doctor, lawyer or minister – a middle class professional – but not a brickie. Well I for one am very pleased, times have changed. This year has been one of the worst in my memory for rain. We have had only three days of sunshine up until seventh of September. Two days in May and yesterday – today it is pishing down yet again. My garden is full of rotting flowers and the roses are dying on the bush, drowned by endless water.

Ian and Margaret Findlay's wedding
Left to right: William Findlay, Jock Findlay, Ian Findlay, Margaret Findlay
(MacAuley), Leonard Findlay

There is something causing this change in the climate but I will leave it to much cleverer people than me to tell us what it is.

I can't help but watch the news and wonder what is going on the world. Thatcher has sounded the death knell for our big industries like shipbuilding, steel and the motor industry. The shale industry is, of course, now a wasteland.

A few years ago, Thatcher's son, Mark, got lost in the Sahara Desert whilst taking part in a car rally. She wept for him in front of the TV cameras, expecting sympathy. Where were her tears for the dead and injured servicemen coming home from the Falklands? Or the miners who have lost their jobs or the shipyards lying silent? Maybe if Thatcher's son takes part in a desert rally in Scotland she could be the co-driver, since she has created this industrial desert.

* * *

It's 1986 and the New Year has just come and gone. When the oil company moved out they sold all the houses to sitting tenants for around £435 in old money – they are now worth £25,000, I can hardly believe it.

When I look around me I see the three big shale tips gone, the refinery demolished and a great industry cast aside in the name of progress. It makes me sad and, in a way, content that I won't be here to see what comes next.
I have come to the conclusion that the people born around the same time as me have witnessed some of the greatest changes at any time in history. From children walking to school in bare feet to men walking on the moon, it is remarkable. I am angry when I read of the disrespect given to the older generation

Jock's son Leonard Findlay with Lena
during his national service in the RAF

Jock's sister Mary Wynne, who ran the local general store for many years

and the end of good manners like standing for a woman if she needs a seat on the bus. I feel that the slavish way Europe and the West follows America in all we do is a terrible mistake.

There is a lot of corruption in our world and it comes right from the top of the political tree. Only this week, Thatcher and her Trade Secretary were before a Parliamentary committee because they have been caught out leaking a letter that was supposed to be confidential. I watched her performance last night and she and Brittan were telling a parcel of lies, not just to the committee but to the whole country.

She talks about wanting to return to 'Victorian values'. Well let me tell you about your so called 'Victorian values'. In the early part of the 20th century, the ordinary worker's money was so valuable to the family that the only toilet paper we had was cut up squares of newspaper bundled together then pierced with a hole and a string threaded through. This was hung on the door handle for use by all the family. Very few could afford to flush money down the shunky buying proper toilet paper – money was far too precious. The main problem with this piece of money-saving thrift was that the newsprint rubbed off when used and your arse was black with reports from the Hearts' or Hibs' match that weekend. There was a famous dance at that time called 'the black bottom' – I always wondered if its origins were in newsprint toilet paper?

* * *

Last month two big events happened. My granddaughter Sheena was married in East Calder Church then to Linburn for the reception. The Reverend Mr Brown conducted the service and many of the male guests were in highland dress. It was a lovely occasion.

In the last few days news has come through from the USSR of a huge nuclear power station disaster at Chernobyl. Apparently, it happened on the 26th April. The fire burned for a long time but it is now out as of today, 8th May, my 71st birthday (my wife Lena's was yesterday she was also 71). Of course, the Western media are having a great time reporting the USSR negatively and saying such a disaster could never happen here – well we'll see about that in time.

* * *

On October 22nd, 1986, I had a fall. I had handed in the artificial leg to be repaired and it came back but wasn't right. This resulted in my good leg giving way and I have torn the tendons from the muscle.

* * *

It's 1987, time is passing so quickly and I haven't wrote in this little book for over a year. It's strange how my memory is slipping and my thoughts and recollections are less clear. My granddaughter Anna gets married on the 22nd of August and this weekend is the show of presents so Lena has been baking.

She has again excelled herself and there is a grand display of goodies to be transported later today to Fauldhouse. I will go up tomorrow but no doubt there will be bugger-all left by the time I get there – she is a great baker and jam maker so the cakes, tarts, scones and pancakes won't last!

* * *

The wedding, a week or so later, was in the chapel and the

Jock with Lena and their son Ian

miners' welfare club. It was huge, with around 300 people there. Anna's husband Jim has got hundreds of relatives, it was a great day but I had to careful with the whisky as my leg has still not fully recovered from the accident last year.

* * *

The raw we live in is mostly occupied by retired people – Lena always said there would be a clearing out of the old folk as we all reached the end of our lives. Well, this week our next door neighbour Mathie Gordon moved out to a Church of Scotland nursing home. Davy Blain at the end of the raw is in hospital having suffered a stroke. Agnes Dick, Flora Martin and Tam Corstorphine are also not in the best of health. We all begin to wonder who will move in if anything happens.

* * *

A few years back I wrote in this book about corruption at the highest level of Government. Since then every month we hear about stockbrokers, company directors and MPs up to their necks in it. I think 95 per cent of the high court judges are paid-up members of the Conservative party and people at the highest level are using their power and influence to feather their own nests and all the time ordinary workers are getting stuffed. This week the news is full of a former MI5 agent who has written his memoirs and has blown the gaff on the dirty tricks used to try and bring down Wilson's Labour Government. Thatcher has spent £2 million in the courts trying to stop the publication of the book. A Government lawyer was even sent to Australia to try and stop publication there. He claimed the Government weren't lying but were being 'economical with the truth'! Has ever an educated man talked as much shite as that? This is the type of country we are now living in. Thatcher's dream of following the Americans has brought us to this. All of the evil we see here has emanated from that country.

* * *

It's now October 23rd 1989 – it is a beautiful autumn day and the leaves are all turning brown, the sun is shining beautifully over the fields, the woods and over the golf course. It is more like spring than autumn. Our front room looks out to the Pentland Hills and the view down to East Calder is magnificent. In my lifetime it has grown from a small village to a much bigger town with lots of new housing.

Jock Findlay with granddaughter Chloe

* * *

2nd March 1994 – my eyesight has really deteriorated and I am unable write anymore. Lena and I are both 79 and my sister Mary is 89.

John 'Jock' Findlay died in St John's hospital in 1999. His wife Lena died in 2005. He was survived by Ian Findlay, my Da (died 14th February 2004) and my uncle Leonard, who still lives in West Lothian.

Note: One feature of Jock's book is that there is very little mention of his disability. The reality is he lost his leg in a motorbike accident when he was in his 20s but he never let this prevent him from working, travelling, enjoying the countryside, driving or his DIY.

Postscript

Neil Findlay

JOCK FINDLAY LIVED through a period of unprecedented and phenomenal change; a time when the country moved from reliance on the horse and cart for transport to mass car ownership and space travel, a time when candles and oil lamps lit homes, to huge oil discoveries in the North Sea, solar power and towns driven by wind energy generation and a time when workers were often tied to the same employer for much of their life to one where job insecurity and zero hours contracts are seen as the norm in many sectors of the economy. It was a time of enormous social and economic change that saw two world wars, the nuclear arms race, mass communications and the development of rapid international travel. Jock marvelled and sometimes despaired at these changes. He took great interest in the technological advances that made life more comfortable for working people but railed against urban sprawl and rapid development over greenbelt, farmland and countryside.

He came from a traditional Scots Presbyterian family where his parents, the Kirk, Masonic Lodge and work influenced his outlook on life. When his son Ian, my Da sought to marry my mum, a devout Catholic of Lithuanian heritage in the early '60s it would have been frowned upon by some but Jock and Lena welcomed Margaret into family with open arms and treated her as one of their own.

Jock's sister Mary owned the general store across from the school and Institute Hall, employing Lena and a whole host

Lena and Mary – both worked in Mary's shop

of local women to work in it. It sold fruit and vegetables, meat and pies, newspapers and the best sweeties in big glass jars – Mary Wynne's shop was a local institution, she ran it up until she retired.

Jock, like most of us, was not without his contradictions. In his later years, he was regularly sent a copy of *The Soviet Weekly* by an old former work colleague, Bob Chelmsford, who lived in Essex, and following holidays to Russia,

Jock Findlay

Yugoslavia, Romania and Bulgaria he became an admirer of the Communist system, but at the same time you would find him in the back room each day checking Ceefax for the performance of his BP shares.

He liked to laugh and play jokes on pals; however, on one occasion he was the victim. Once the same pal from Essex sent him a box of 'quick growing grass seed' and asked him to spread it on his manicured lawn spelling out the words 'HOME RULE FOR ENGLAND.' He was then to take a photo of it when it had grown and sent it to Bob. Once done, the grass was to be cut back reinstating the pristine lawn. 'The quick grown grass seed' turned out to be lime and immediately

Jock and Lena

burned the message hard into the grass – it remained there for all to see for the next 9 months.

As they reached their late 70s and 80s, Jock, Lena and his sister Mary met each Sunday for lunch at Jock and Lena's house in the raws. Roast beef and trimmings were always followed by home baking, pancakes and scones with Lena's jam made from fruit from cousin Ronald's farm down the Clyde Valley. Woe betide anyone who interrupted the next hour as they sat and laughed helplessly watching the exploits of Compo, Clegg, Foggy and Norah Batty in *Last of the Summer Wine*. That is how I love to remember Jock, with Lena and Mary – laughing together, in a welcoming home, in the community that meant so much to them and that they genuinely loved.

His was a good life, shaped by hard work, respect, thrift, family and community. Jock Findlay my Granda RIP.

Jock in the Middle East

JOCK SPENT SOME time in Abadan in the Middle East following the war. He worked in the emerging oil industry. One the pages that follow are some of the postcards he sent home.

Jock in Arabic dress during his time working in the Middle East

Dear Ian,

Do you know what is on the picture? They are camels, one is getting its dinner while the other two are looking for more. See they have long legs and large feet. They carry their drivers across the sand and can run very fast. They eat an awful lot of meal and drink a lot of water.

Lots of love Daddy XXXX

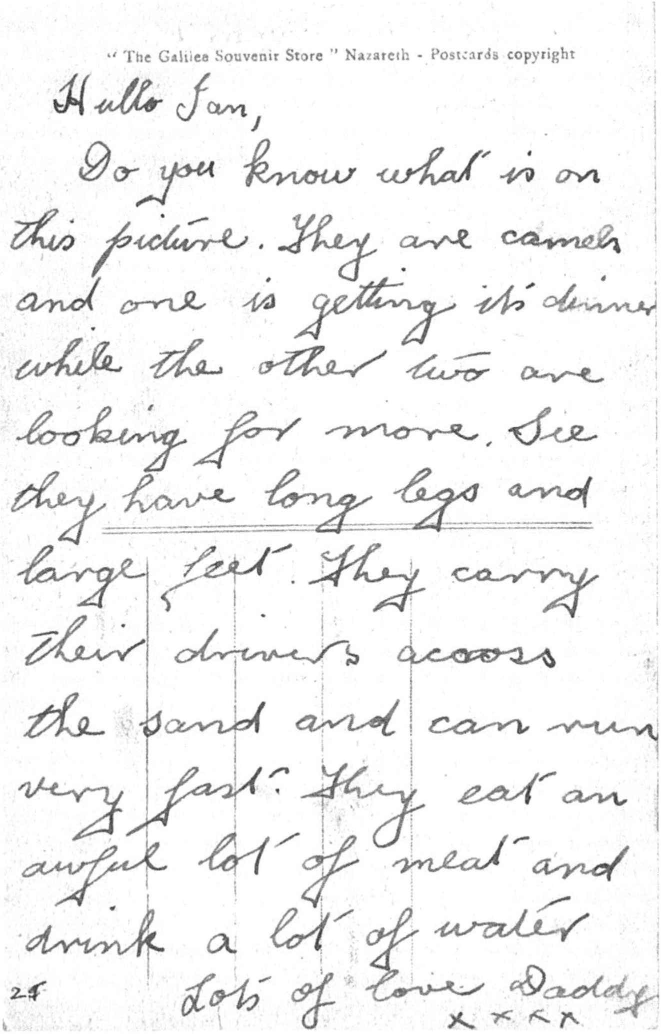

" The Galilee Souvenir Store " Nazareth - Postcards copyright

Hullo Jan,

Do you know what is on this picture. They are camels and one is getting it's dinner while the other two are looking for more. See they have long legs and large feet. They carry their drivers across the sand and can run very fast. They eat an awful lot of meat and drink a lot of water

Lots of love Daddy

x x x x

Jerusalem — Sheep and Shepherds in the Valley of the Jordan (× Mount of Temptation) 621 d

Hello Ian,

Are you being a clever boy for your Mammy too. I hope
you are and don't get into mischief. This is a picture of the
sheep and the shepherds. They do not wear the same dress
as we do but have long beards and live in tents. There is a
lot of sand you can play with here and the sea is coloured
blue and the sun shines all day.

Lots of love Daddy

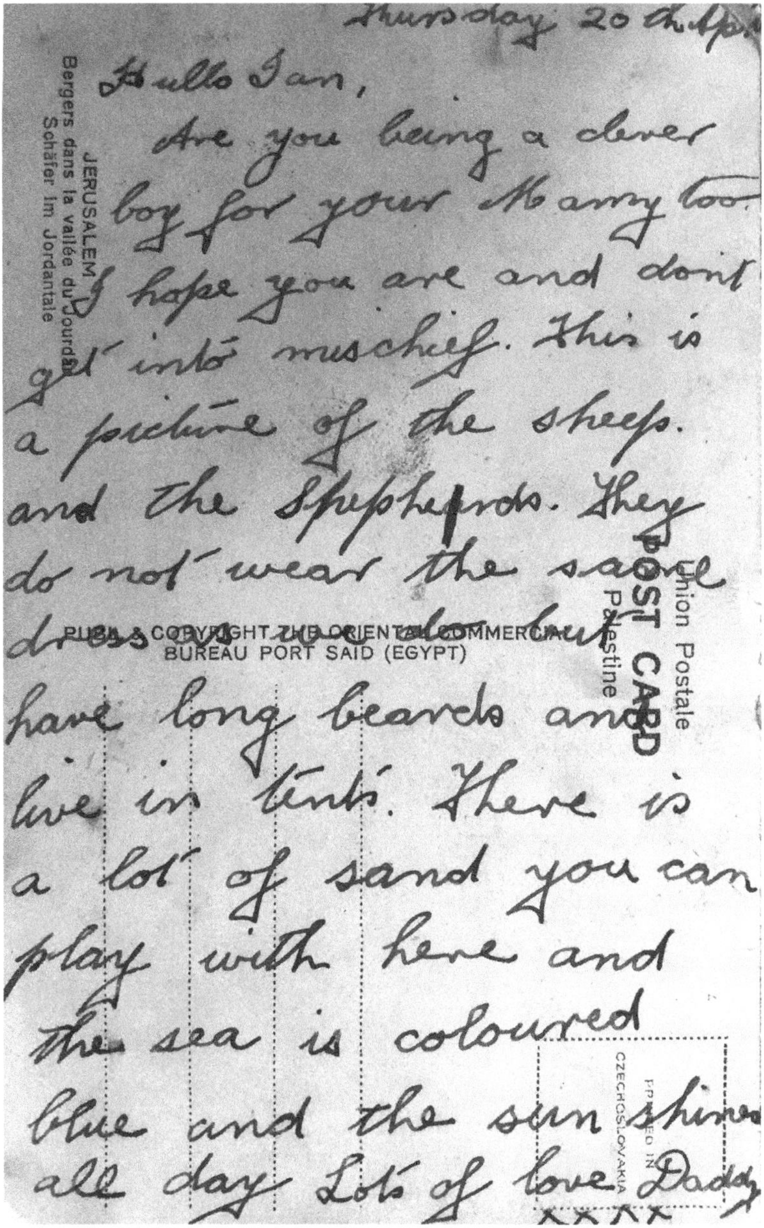

Thursday 20 th April

Hullo Ian,

Are you being a clever boy for your Mammy too. I hope you are and dont get into mischief. This is a picture of the sheep. and the Shepherds. They do not wear the same dress. They have long beards and live in tents. There is a lot of sand you can play with here and the sea is coloured blue and the sun shines all day Lots of love Daddy

xxxx

TO: MRS. & MR WM. FINDLAY,
140 SOUTH VILLAGE,
PUMPHERSTON,
MIDCALDER,
MIDLOTHIAN,
SCOTLAND.

Write the message very plainly below this line.

Dear Mother & Father   Sender's Address 7/133/1 A.I.O.C. ABADAN

I hope this finds you in the best of health,
I am getting on fine here and enjoying life Date 7th August 1946
to the full. Have been looking for your letter for months now and
I am afraid it must be lost as I have had one from Lena's mother
and she wrote after you. How is all our family getting on and I
hope you are taking good care of Wull's fortune earner. Lena was
saying in her graphs that Mary had been at Crossford with her
for Jeut. That means you will be kept very busy for a week or
two now, making jam. I am always wondering if my father has
retired yet and he must be giving that dog a very good training
according to the amount of walking he does with it. Lena tells
me all about it. you know. Well all the local lads are getting
on fine and are enjoying the best of health. The worst of the
heat is past now and I am pleased to say I came through it
well. When I first came here I was in tents for about five days
until I got accommodation and believe me anyone who can
stick that can stick anything here. There were no fans
in them and it was very warm in April and May. I am
pleased to know Mary and Jam go so often to Seafield and
it will always be good company for Lena. Look after yourselves
and the time will not be long in passing until I get home.
Take care of Lena and the boys for me. Jock.

This space should not be used.

MAKE SURE THAT THE ADDRESS IS WRITTEN IN LARGE BLOCK LETTERS IN THE PANEL ABOVE

94

7th August 1944

Dear Mother & Father,

*I hope this finds you in the best of health, I am getting on
fine here and am enjoying life to the full. Have been looking
for your letter for months now and afraid it must be lost
as I have had one from Lena's mother and she wrote after
you. How are all the family getting on and I hope you are
looking after Wull's fortune earner. Lena has been saying
in her graph that Mary had been at Crossford with her
for fruit. That means you will be busy for a week or two
now, making jam. I am always wondering if my father
has retired yet and he must be giving that dog a very good
training according to the amount of walking he does with
it. Lena tells me all about it you know. Well all the local
lads are getting on fine and are enjoying the best of health.
The worst of the heat is past now and I am pleased to say
I came through it well. When I first came here I was in
tents for about five days until I got accommodation and
believe me anyone who can stick that can stick anything
here. There were no fans in them and it was very warm in
April and May. I am pleased to know Mary and Tam go so
often to Seafield and it will be always be good company for
Lena. Look after yourselves and the time will not be long in
passing until I get home.*

Take care of Lena and the boys for me.

Jock

Write address in large BLOCK letters wholly within this panel)))⟶

The address must NOT be typewritten.

TO:— Mr & Mrs. Wm. FINDLAY,
140 SOUTH VILLAGE,
PUMPHERSTON,
MID LOTHIAN,
SCOTLAND.

جدول اسم وعنوان
المرسلة الرسالة بحروف
كبيرة و بلدته في حينها
للمن :— .
ولا يجوز ان تكون هذه
للآلة الطابعة

Write the message very plainly below this line.

٠٠٠٤٤٣٩

Sender's Address: % A.I.O.C. ABADAN   اسم وعنوان المرسل

Dear Mother & Father,

I hope this finds you both well and in good health. I am getting along fine here. The weather doesn't give me much trouble at all. Although it can be damned warm sometimes. I have had a day off work today as I have been moving to get my quarters painted. This is the third time I have flitted in 3 months. Dick Martin is arriving tonight and I am going to meet him off the launch. I am looking forward to getting Lena's photograph and to hear how you are all getting on. I am pleased to hear from Mary that you have wrote to me, and I will probably receive it in two months time from the day you posted it. Maybe Mary could write me a graph once a week, and what about Tam? Tell Will to be careful how he handles that dog as he will have plenty of friends once it starts to run. I hope he takes it to Seafield now and again as it will be good exercise for both. I have an Arab whose name is Mahmud Ali, but he doesn't know how to spell his name and neither do I. Anyhow he cleans my place out and goes for my messages, about the only thing he omits is to put me to bed. There are plenty of Scotsmen here and soon it will be Pumpherston Rows if they keep coming like this. There are 8 off us here now. Take good care of yourselves and look after Lena and the boys for me. The time here passes very quickly.   Jock.

Date 5th July 1944

This space should not be used.   لا يجوز استعمال هذا القسم من الاستمارة
MAKE SURE THAT THE ADDRESS IS WRITTEN IN LARGE BLOCK LETTERS IN THE PANEL ABOVE

5th July 1944

Dear Mother & Father,

I hope this finds you both in good health. I am getting along fine here. The weather doesn't give me much trouble at all. Although it can be damned hot at sometimes. I have had a day off work today as I have been meaning to get my quarters painted. This is the third time I have flitted in 3 months. Chick Martin is arriving today and I am going to meet him off the launch. I am looking forward to getting Lena's photograph and to hear how you are all getting on. I am pleased to hear from Mary that you have wrote to me, and I will probably get it in two months time from the day you posted it. Maybe Mary could write me a graph once a week, and what about Tam? Tell Wull to be careful how he handles that dog as he will have plenty of friends when it starts to run. I hope he takes it to Seafield now and again as it will be good exercise for both. I have an Arab whose name is Muhamid Ali, but he doesn't know how to spell his name and neither do I. Anyhow he cleans my place out and goes for my messages, about the only thing he omits is to put me to bed. There are plenty Scotsmen here and soon it will be like Pumpherston Raws if they keep coming like this. There are 8 of us here now. Take good care of yourselves and look after Lena and the boys for me. The time here passes very quickly. Jock

The Writing Discovered on the Bath Panel

John B Findlay 15th March Aged 63
Renovated this house in the year 1978 by himself and it has
taken a damned long time to complete.

I worked with the old Pumpherston Oil Co Ltd as a plumber
and lead burner from 1929 when I started my apprenticeship
under William Brown, who had a wooden pin leg, and I am
damned if I didn't finish up with one leg too. The village in
those days was a lovely place to reside in. The houses had only
one bedroom, a kitchen that is now called the living room
and a scullery and toilet or closet as we called it in those days.

The woods and surrounding farmlands were lovely to look upon
and the walks that surrounded the village were so quiet and
beautiful in the summer days. Those were the days before the
new town of Livingston was developed. There used to be three
ponds where swans used to nest and rear their young ones, also
water hens and coots and in spring the frogs would cover part
of the pond with spawn and we used to watch them hatch into
tadpoles. The scent of heather and clover on a warm summer
day filled the air and bees were in abundance, we scarcely see
them nowadays in this locality. The golf course had at one time
a large opencast left from working the shale deposits and they
were a happy playground for us when we were children.

There were quite a few local characters around the place,
Cockie Flucker was the 'scaffy' or street cleaner and woe
betide you if Cockie saw you drop a piece of paper on the
street. The sheughs or gutters in front of the houses were
swept every day.

Around the village there was such names as Clay Road, Rosy Lane, the Loan, the Mair Road – up the Mair and doon the Mair was a great walk in those days, there was also the Craw flee and the Hutton line. I used to watch the shale miners come home, they wore moleskin trousers with nicky tams below the knee and tacketty boots on, their wives used to knit longjohns from heavy pink wool.

Many a stormy night I have heard my mother say when the wind was howling and rain lashing down 'God help the men on the tip on a night like this.' The tips of spent shale covered acres of ground and must have been at least 700 feet high. The hutches of shale were emptied at the top into the prevailing west wind – you can imagine the tipman emptying a ton of spent shale with the wind throwing dust and fumes and small pieces of shale over the place. These men must have had one hell of a job. They reckon that there was over 22 million tonnes on one tip alone.

On a winter's night we would be in the house early, coal fire blazing and oil lamp burning, my mother knitting, my sister doing crochet work, my father reading the paper and my brothers reading books by Zane Grey. Life was simple, we didn't have much money but we had a peaceful existence.

We were never really church people but we were God-fearing just the same. I always remember when the Minister was on his rounds we used to make a dash for the door and leave my mother to make all the excuses for us.

I must tell you of the worthy in the village who had a spell in hospital. My wife was asking how his health was and if he was feeling well enough now. 'Well you know Mrs Findlay, there is only one thing worries me now and that is I cannot break the habit of counting my money and I have since discovered the reason for this is that they told me when I had a blood transfusion the donor's blood belonged to the Midcalder bank manager.'

I hope this will be of interest to read for whoever finds this board. I only did it to pass the time, as time surely is passing me.

The best of luck to the finder. JB Findlay

Pumpherston Housing

Theodore K Irvine, Report on the Housing Conditions
in the Scottish Shale Field, 1914 (describing collectively
Pumpherston North and Pumpherston South Villages)

THE PUMPHERSTON OIL COMPANY own 220 houses in this village,
which is situated about one mile north from Mid Calder. These
houses are built of brick, and rough-cast or cement-washed. In a
number of cases, however, the back of the house, which faces the
drying greens, is neither rough-cast nor cement-washed, and this
presents an unfinished appearance. There are about 173 houses
consisting of room (12 ft by 11 ft, also bed-recess and press),
kitchen (14.5 ft by 11 ft, also two bed-recesses), scullery (7.5 ft
by 6 ft) with sink and water-closet. A washhouse is provided for
every four tenants. The rental is 2/6 to 2/9 per week, inclusive of
rates. In the case of 36 of these houses, the room and kitchen are
approximately 11 ft by 16.5 ft each, and the scullery is 10 ft 5
inches by 7 ft 8 inches, which contains sink, set-in tub, boiler, and
water-closet. There are 19 houses consisting of three apartments,
and all conveniences as above, let at from 4/- to 4/9 per week.
Then there are 27 single-apartment houses, with scullery and
water-closet, let at 1/6 per week, inclusive of rates. Some 60
houses are built back to back. A good supply of gravitation
water is obtained, and a good drainage system exists. The refuse
is collected daily by the Company, from dustbins provided to
each tenant. The gardens are made good use of by the workers,
and present a good appearance in the season. An Institute, with
a good library and hall, exists. There is also a bowling green in
the centre of the village, for all of which the workers subscribe
weekly. The total number of houses in Pumpherston district is
260, and in Mid Calder 335, with an approximate population
in the two districts of 2,990 persons.

The raws today

Luath Press Limited

committed to publishing well written books worth reading

LUATH PRESS takes its name from Robert Burns, whose little collie Luath (*Gael.*, swift or nimble) tripped up Jean Armour at a wedding and gave him the chance to speak to the woman who was to be his wife and the abiding love of his life. Burns called one of the 'Twa Dogs' Luath after Cuchullin's hunting dog in Ossian's *Fingal*. Luath Press was established in 1981 in the heart of Burns country, and is now based a few steps up the road from Burns' first lodgings on Edinburgh's Royal Mile. Luath offers you distinctive writing with a hint of unexpected pleasures.

Most bookshops in the UK, the US, Canada, Australia, New Zealand and parts of Europe, either carry our books in stock or can order them for you. To order direct from us, please send a £sterling cheque, postal order, international money order or your credit card details (number, address of cardholder and expiry date) to us at the address below. Please add post and packing as follows: UK – £1.00 per delivery address; overseas surface mail – £2.50 per delivery address; overseas airmail – £3.50 for the first book to each delivery address, plus £1.00 for each additional book by airmail to the same address. If your order is a gift, we will happily enclose your card or message at no extra charge.

Luath Press Limited
543/2 Castlehill
The Royal Mile
Edinburgh EH1 2ND
Scotland
Telephone: +44 (0)131 225 4326 (24 hours)
Email: sales@luath.co.uk
Website: www.luath.co.uk